CLIMATE CHANGE

GLOBAL CITIZENS: ENVIRONMENTALISM

Published in the United States of America by Cherry Lake Publishing
Ann Arbor, Michigan
www.cherrylakepublishing.com

Content Adviser: Michael Rockett MS, Natural resources

Reading Adviser: Marla Conn MS, Ed., Literacy specialist, Read-Ability, Inc.

Photo Credits: © idiz/Shutterstock.com, cover, 1; © andyparker72/Shutterstock.com, 5; © Vitoriano Junior/Shutterstock.com, 6; © vladimir salman/Shutterstock.com, 8; © thechatat/Shutterstock.com, 10; © Bernhard Staehli/Shutterstock.com, 13; © Rich Carey/Shutterstock.com, 14; © Andaman/Shutterstock.com, 16; © Bastian Kienitz/Shutterstock.com, 19; © otomobil/Shutterstock.com, 20; © Africa Studio/Shutterstock.com, 22; © Leonid Eremeychuk/Shutterstock.com, 25; © 29september/Shutterstock.com, 26; © TuiPhotoEngineer/Shutterstock.com, 28

Library of Congress Cataloging-in-Publication Data
Names: Labrecque, Ellen.
Title: Climate change / Ellen Labrecque.
Description: Ann Arbor : Cherry Lake Publishing, 2017. | Series: Global citizens: environmentalism |
    Audience: Grade 4 to 6. | Includes bibliographical references and index.
Identifiers: LCCN 2016058618| ISBN 9781634728690 (hardcover) | ISBN 9781634729581 (pdf) |
    ISBN 9781534100473 (pbk.) | ISBN 9781534101364 (hosted ebook)
Subjects: LCSH: Environmentalism—Juvenile literature. | Climatic changes—Juvenile literature. |
    Climatic changes—Social aspects—Juvenile literature.
Classification: LCC GE195.5 .L33 2017 | DDC 363.738/74—dc23
LC record available at https://lccn.loc.gov/2016058618

Cherry Lake Publishing would like to acknowledge the work of the Partnership for 21st Century Learning.
Please visit www.p21.org for more information.

Printed in the United States of America
Corporate Graphics

ABOUT THE AUTHOR

Ellen Labrecque has written over 100 books for children. She is passionate about being a friend to the environment and taking care of our planet. She lives in Pennsylvania with her husband, Jeff, and her two young "editors," Sam and Juliet. She loves running, hiking, and reading.

TABLE OF CONTENTS

CHAPTER 1

History: Weather Is Always Changing 4

CHAPTER 2

Geography: Climate Change at the Top of the World 12

CHAPTER 3

Civics: Can Anything Be Done? 18

CHAPTER 4

Economics: Money to Stop Climate Change.................................24

THINK ABOUT IT... 30
FOR MORE INFORMATION...31
GLOSSARY 32
INDEX... 32

History: Weather Is Always Changing

Environmentalism is a big word. But its meaning is simple. Practicing environmentalism means being a friend of Earth and all its creatures. Environmentalists want to keep our air healthy, our land clean, and our water fresh. They want to take care of our plants and animals by making sure our planet remains a safe place to live. Some environmentalists focus on encouraging people to stop polluting. Others encourage people to **recycle**. One of the most important environmental jobs is to teach people about **climate change**.

The Story of Climate Change

Earth has been around for about 4.5 billion years. Throughout all these years, the **climate** has always been changing. During

Many people care about protecting Earth from climate change.

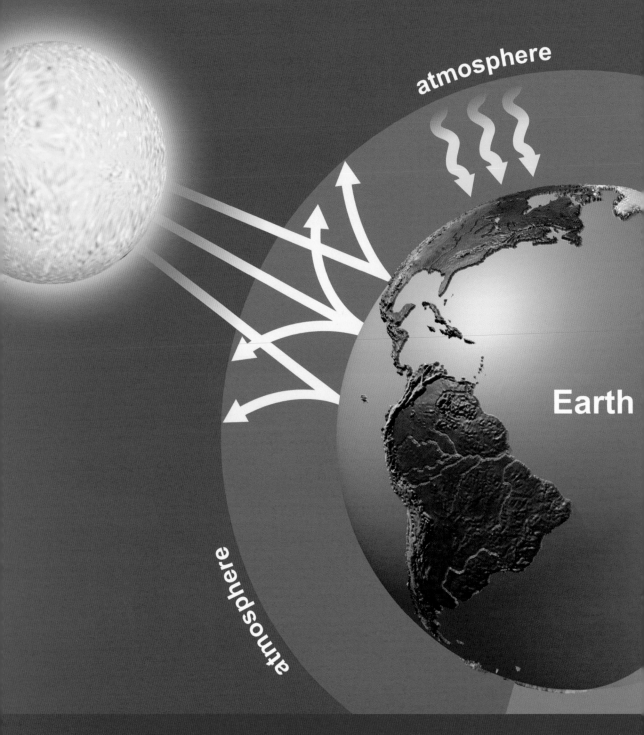

Sun

atmosphere

Earth

atmosphere

The greenhouse effect is part of Earth's natural way of keeping us warm.

some time periods, the planet is hotter. Other times the planet is covered entirely in ice. But researchers believe that today's climate change is different. Studies indicate that human actions may be contributing to climate change.

Scientists have known about climate change for almost 200 years. In 1827, French mathematician Joseph Fourier learned that Earth's atmosphere traps heat from the sun like a greenhouse. Today, we call this the **greenhouse effect**. Atmosphere is the air surrounding Earth. It is made up of different gases, including nitrogen, oxygen, argon, and carbon dioxide. These gases work together. If there were no atmosphere, the sun's heat would bounce off Earth and head back into space. Earth would be freezing cold, and nothing would survive.

In 1896, Swedish scientist Svante Arrhenius began to think the atmosphere was changing. He thought that there was more carbon dioxide in it than there should be. In 1958, scientist Charles David Keeling proved Arrhenius right. By collecting data, Keeling proved that there was 10 percent more carbon dioxide in the atmosphere than just a century before. Carbon dioxide is a gas that absorbs the heat from the sun. The more carbon dioxide in the atmosphere, the hotter our temperatures become.

Relying too much on fossil fuels can harm the planet.

This excess carbon dioxide has been caused by industrial activity. Factories, cars, and pollution from our **landfills** spill carbon dioxide into the atmosphere. And the **population** has dramatically increased. In 1804, more than 1 billion people lived on Earth. Today, that number is over 7 billion. These people rely on **fossil fuels** like coal, oil, and natural gas which also contribute to the excess carbon dioxide in the atmosphere.

Global Warming

In 1975, scientist Wallace Broecker came up with the term **global warming**. This term means that our planet is getting warmer because of the gases being released into the atmosphere. The average temperature around the world has increased by about 1 degree Fahrenheit (0.5 degree Celsius) since 1900. 1 degree doesn't sound like a lot, but studies indicate that prior to 1900, a change in 1 or 2 degrees Fahrenheit (0.5 or 1 degree Celsius) took 10,000 years. The 10 hottest years on record have all happened in the last 20 years.

Global warming isn't just about temperatures getting warmer. This warming causes weather pattern changes, too. Storms become bigger, **droughts** happen more frequently, and areas not

Severe droughts are drying up entire rivers and streams.

prone to flooding suddenly experience an increase. Because of these consistent and repeating patterns in the weather, people now call global warming "climate change." The weather and climate are different. Weather is the conditions outside over a short period of time. Climate is a measure of the weather over a long period of time.

Developing Questions

Small actions, like riding your bike or turning off the lights when you leave a room, can make a big impact on climate change. Why do you think this is? What are other ways you can fight climate change?

A close-ended question is a question that can be answered with a simple yes or no. An open-ended question is one that needs more thought when answering. The questions above are meant to be open-ended questions. They are meant to make you think about ways you can help the planet rather than just answering yes or no.

CHAPTER 2

Geography: Climate Change at the Top of the World

Signs of climate change can be found all over the planet. But the **Arctic** is changing most of all. Snow and ice are melting there at a record pace. It is warming twice as fast as the rest of the planet. Ice and snow reflect the sun's rays back into space. This is called the **albedo effect**. Without the snow and ice, more of the sun's heat is absorbed, making it even warmer.

Polar Bears

Scientists estimate that about 26,000 polar bears live in the Arctic. These bears live on the ice while they hunt for seals to eat. By 2080, the ice in the Arctic is expected to have completely disappeared during the summer months. Some bears have

Research shows that Antarctica's ice is rapidly melting.

These homes are at risk of being destroyed if water continues to rise.

drowned trying to swim too far to the next big patch of ice. Without sea ice, polar bears can't hunt. If they can't hunt, they can't survive. This could mean the bears are in danger of going **extinct**.

Rising and Warming Waters

The ice caps melting in the Arctic causes sea levels to rise. It also makes water warmer. By the end of this century, scientists predict that sea levels could rise by as much as 2 feet (61 centimeters). This means some coastal areas and islands would disappear, along with people's homes. Islands that could disappear are Bermuda and the Bahamas. Some low-lying coastal cities, like Miami, New York City, Los Angeles, and Tokyo, Japan, could all be threatened.

Miami is already dealing with rising sea levels. Sometimes seawater rises up through their drains. They call this "sunny day flooding." To combat the surging tide, the city has raised roads and installed pumps. But these solutions will only last for 40 to 50 years.

The warming water is causing fish to lose their homes, too. **Coral reefs** are home to thousands of different species of fish. But the reefs can't survive warm waters. When the waters get too warm, the coral reefs die and leave the fish homeless.

Many fish depend on coral reefs to survive.

Within the next 30 years, over 30 percent of all coral reefs on Earth may be lost.

Droughts

A drought means people do not have enough water to drink or to water their crops. As many places get too much water, some places will not get enough. When temperatures rise, **moisture evaporates** from the land, leaving less water behind. Areas in southern Africa and southern India are all receiving less **precipitation** because of climate change. Deserts around the world are also expanding. People have to prepare for more periods of drought in the future by using less water now.

Gathering and Evaluating Sources

Different types of maps show different things. A political map shows the borders of countries and states. Physical maps show landscape features, such as mountains and rivers. Some environmentalists use a Risk Zone Map. This map shows areas of the world that are at risk due to sea levels rising. Check out this map by visiting www.sealevel.climatecentral.org/maps.

CHAPTER 3

Civics: Can Anything Be Done?

In order to stop climate change from getting worse, scientists think the world needs to cut back on burning fossil fuels. This is not easy, though. People burn fossil fuels when they drive cars and trucks. Buses, trains, ships, and airplanes also need fossil fuels to run. We use oil and gas to heat our homes, schools, and stores. Coal is burned to run power plants and major factories. How do we change?

Different Kinds of Energy

Scientists want to promote more renewable energy. Renewable energy is energy that is produced from **renewable resources**. One form of renewable energy is wind power. Power from the wind can be turned into energy to power our electricity and heat

These are wind turbines in California.

our homes. **Wind turbines** do the job of capturing the wind without polluting the air.

There are still challenges with wind energy, however. Scientists haven't figured out a way to store the energy from wind in large amounts. It is also expensive. Many factors go into the cost, like building, installing, and operating these turbines. But work is being done to fix these problems. Scientists hope that by 2020, 10 percent of the world's electricity will be wind powered.

Another way we can use renewable energy is by driving electric cars. Electric cars run on rechargeable batteries instead of

More and more people are driving electric cars around the world.

Top Five Countries with the Most Wind Turbines

1. China
2. United States
3. Germany
4. Spain
5. India

gasoline. The country of Norway is leading the electric car charge. Twenty-four percent of its cars are now electric. One way that Norway is able to encourage people to use electric cars is by setting up charging stations all over the country. Instead of stopping at a gas station to fill up, people stop and charge up.

Other types of natural and renewable energy sources are solar (getting energy from the sun), hydropower (getting energy from water), and geothermal (getting energy from below Earth's surface). These types of energy are used all over the world, but much more could still be done. Scientists believe that if we continue to use fossil fuels at our current rate, there won't be any left in just 100 years. Renewable energy, however, can last forever.

Agreeing to Change

China and the United States have the highest carbon emissions of all countries. In 1997 in Kyoto, Japan, leaders from countries all over the world met to talk about climate change. The idea was for countries to commit to lowering their greenhouse gas emissions. But the United States, despite being a top polluter, didn't agree to the Kyoto Protocol. US officials thought that

Riding your bike to school can help cut pollution.

cutting greenhouse gas emissions would lead to factory workers losing their jobs. They also thought people should be able to drive their cars as much as they wanted.

In 2015, government leaders from around the world met again to discuss climate change. More than 190 nations gathered in Paris, France. This time, the United States pledged to reduce its emissions by 28 percent by 2025.

Developing Claims and Using Evidence

The United States only has 4 percent of the world's population but emits about 16 percent of the world's greenhouse gases. Do you think the United States should have committed to the Kyoto Protocol? How about the Paris Agreement? Can you find evidence supporting this and evidence against this? Using evidence you found, form your own opinion on the Kyoto Protocol and the Paris Agreement.

CHAPTER 4

Economics: Money to Stop Climate Change

Scientists estimate that it would cost trillions of dollars for the world to make the switch from burning fossil fuels to using alternative energy. This sounds like a lot of money. But research indicates that continuing to burn fossil fuels would cost even more. How should we invest this money?

Research

Scientists are researching a new type of technology called carbon capturing. This is a system that would grab the carbon dioxide coming from factories and power plants before it goes into the atmosphere.

Oil refineries burn fossil fuels. This contributes to climate change.

Trees and other plants can slow down climate change.

Tree Planting

Trees absorb carbon dioxide. The more we plant, the less carbon dioxide goes into the atmosphere. Even if we don't plant more trees, we should protect the trees we currently have growing in our forests. Deforestation, or the permanent removal of forests, can contribute to climate change.

Jobs and Money

Working to stop climate change also brings jobs and money into countries. China creates more "green collar" jobs than anywhere else in the world. It has more than 3.4 million people working throughout the entire renewable energy industry.

Communicating Conclusions

Before reading this book, did you know about climate change? Now that you know more, why do you think this is an important issue? Share your knowledge about climate change and the importance of being a friend to Earth. Every week, look up different organizations that work to stop climate change. Share what you learn with friends at school or with family at home.

Scientists and engineers develop and advance renewable energy technologies.

Germany leads Europe with 370,000 of its people working to stop climate change.

The United States leads the world in solar energy jobs. It has close to 209,000 people working in this industry and hopes to increase this number by 20 percent every year.

Taking Informed Action

Do you want to help stop climate change? There are many ways you can get involved and many different organizations you can explore. Check them out online. Here are three to start your search:

- A Student's Guide to Global Climate Change: Read this student guide from the Environmental Protection Agency (EPA).
- Real Climate: Learn about climate change from scientists.
- The Nature Conservancy Carbon Calculator: Calculate your own **carbon footprint**!

Think About It

There are more than 7 billion people living on Earth. It is estimated that by 2050, 9.7 billion people will live here. Population growth and climate change are linked together. The more people on our planet, the more people will need fossil fuels to heat their homes and drive their cars. Educators believe that providing education about climate change is the first step to a cleaner future. Why is it important to understand the relationship between population and climate change? What are ways we can solve the problem of climate change? Use the data you find in your research to support your argument.

For More Information

FURTHER READING

Arnold, Caroline, and Jamie Hogan (illustrator). *A Warmer World*. Watertown, MA: Charlesbridge, 2012.

Espejo, Roman. *Adaptation and Climate Change*. Detroit: Greenhaven Press, 2013.

Johnson, Rebecca L. *Understanding Global Warming*. Minneapolis: Lerner Publications, 2009.

WEB SITES

Alliance to Save Energy
www.ase.org
This is a great place to learn how you can help fight climate change.

National Geographic—Climate Connections
http://ngm.nationalgeographic.com/climateconnections
Find all kinds of information about climate change.

Natural Resources Defense Council—Global Warming 101
www.nrdc.org/stories/global-warming-101
Learn from experts around the world about global warming.

GLOSSARY

albedo effect (al-BEE-doh ih-FEKT) measure of how much of the sun's heat is reflected back into space

Arctic (AHRK-tik) the North Pole region or area

carbon footprint (KAHR-buhn FUT-print) a measure of the amount of carbon dioxide produced by a person, object, or organization and released into the atmosphere

climate (KLYE-mit) weather patterns over a long period of time

climate change (KLYE-mit CHAYNJ) a change in normal weather patterns over a long period of time

coral reefs (KOR-uhl REEFS) ridges of rock under the sea made from coral

droughts (DROUTS) periods of dry weather

environmentalism (en-vye-ruhn-MEN-tuhl-iz-uhm) working to protect the air, water, animals, and plants from pollution and other harmful things

evaporates (ih-VAP-uh-rayts) changes from a liquid or solid into a vapor or mist

extinct (ik-STINGT) no longer exists or has died out

fossil fuels (FAH-suhl FYOOLZ) oil, coal, and gas formed from the remains of animals and plants that died and decayed millions of years ago

global warming (GLOH-buhl WORM-ing) the warming of the earth's surface and air caused by an increase of carbon dioxide in the atmosphere

greenhouse effect (GREEN-hous ih-FEKT) the natural process of heat being trapped in the atmosphere rather than being released into space

landfills (LAND-filz) large outdoor areas used to dump garbage

moisture (MOIS-cher) a small amount of liquid, especially water

population (pahp-yuh-LAY-shuhn) the number of people in one place

precipitation (prih-sip-ih-TAY-shuhn) moisture that falls from the sky, including rain, sleet, snow, and hail

recycle (ree-SYE-kuhl) to break something down in order to make something new from it

renewable resources (rih-NOO-uh-buhl REE-sors-iz) natural power, such as wind, that will never be used up and can be used again and again

wind turbines (WIND TUR-binz) machines that capture the wind, which eventually is converted to energy

INDEX

albedo effect, 12
alternative energy, 24
Antarctica, 13
Arctic, 12–13, 15
atmosphere, 7, 9, 24, 27

carbon dioxide, 7, 9, 24, 27
climate change
  in the Arctic, 12–13, 15
  causes, 9
  economics, 24–29
  what can be done, 18–23, 26, 27
  what it is, 4–11

coral reefs, 15–17

deserts, 17
droughts, 9–10, 17

electric cars, 19–21
electricity, 18, 19
energy, 18–21
environmentalism, 4

fossil fuels, 8, 9, 18, 21, 24, 25, 30

gases, 7, 9
geography, 12–17
geothermal power, 21
global warming, 9, 11

greenhouse effect, 6, 7
greenhouse gases, 21, 23

hydropower, 21

ice and snow, 12–13, 15

jobs, 27, 29

Kyoto Protocol, 21

Paris Agreement, 23
polar bears, 12, 15
precipitation, 17

renewable energy, 18–21, 28
Risk Zone Maps, 17

sea levels, 13–15
solar energy, 21, 29
"sunny day flooding," 15

trees, 26, 27

weather, 11
wind power, 18–19, 20